THE FOUR ELEMENTS OF DESIGN

INTERIORS INSPIRED BY AIR, WATER, EARTH, AND FIRE

THE FOUR ELEMENTS OF DESIGN
INTERIORS INSPIRED BY AIR, WATER, EARTH, AND FIRE

WORDS AND PHOTOGRAPHS BY VICENTE WOLF
WRITTEN WITH LINDA O'KEEFFE
FOREWORD BY MARGARET RUSSELL

RIZZOLI
NEW YORK
New York · Paris · London · Milan

VICENTE WOLF

I DEDICATE THIS BOOK TO MATTHEW YEE, JANE EPSTEIN, AND TIM CORRIGAN.

TABLE OF CONTENTS

FOREWORD

By Margaret Russell

Editor in Chief, *Architectural Digest*

It makes perfect sense that Vicente Wolf would write a book focused on interiors inspired by the four classical elements—they are the very essence of his personal character and point of view. In our twenty-five years of friendship, I've always known him to have a remarkably grounded sensibility, like earth; he is as passionate and vital as fire, as clear and fluid as water, and as imaginative and carefree as air. Spiritual yet pragmatic, he has always been able to find that perfect balance between an intellectual and emotional connection to his clients and their spaces and the practical imperative to create interiors that will work for them and their families.

But the most important aspect of Vicente's work is far less easy to define—how it feels to be in one of his rooms. Each space is an escape, a refuge. Take his seaside retreat in Montauk, New York, not far from where I've summered since I was a child. I have visited him there many times and know it well; it is truly one of my most favorite places. The breeze blows and wind chimes jangle, muffled by the roar of the surf. Walls and ceilings are lacquered a glossy snow-white; floors of randomly laid stone welcome bare feet; deep upholstery is covered in cool canvas and scattered with cushions in limpid blues and greens. Everywhere your eye lands, there is beauty: leafy branches cut from the garden, a Buddha fragment, black-and-white photography, and luxe furnishings leavened with rustic objects, all complemented by gorgeous ocean views.

Sparked by the strength and grace of this sublime natural setting, Vicente has made a home for himself that is a microcosm of his widely publicized projects, whether a Manhattan penthouse or a suburban Georgian Revival. His work is as polished as it is idiosyncratic, filled with belongings that reflect his clients' beliefs, their interests, their goals, and, indeed, their lives. To me, that's interior design at its very best—personal, profound, and unmistakably you.

INTRODUCTION

The most successful interiors soothe the senses and allow us to be ourselves. They reflect our personalities, desires, and aspirations. They indicate where we've been; they reveal where we may be headed. Whenever I walk into a well-designed room, I'm transformed in some way—always for the better. Whether the room calms, stimulates, comforts, balances, relaxes me, or revs me up, I'm always emotionally engaged.

But then, my surroundings have always engaged me emotionally. I recall having an experiential relationship with objects and environments from the earliest age, and I always felt nourished by nature, whether I was in the mountains, forest, or desert. I'm equally at home in cities, so it's no surprise that I'm a frequent traveler, one who's inspired equally by the mundane and the exotic. The prospect of any new adventure invigorates me, as I know it will oil my creative wheels and expand my frame of reference.

Luckily, my chosen profession allows me to incorporate my experiences into the backdrops I create for people in which they can live the lives they love. My clients' personal experiences, as well as their needs, are always in the foreground when I design. And if, let's say, they consider a walk on the beach to be the height of relaxation, then I distill the essence of their recollections of such walks into the decor of a living room or a bedroom with the help of colors, textures, and shapes. I can translate the DNA of a cresting wave into a serpentine-shaped sofa. I'll include driftwood and soothing shades of watery blue; nubby raw silk that emulates the gritty texture of wet sand; and a wall color inspired by the astounding range of grays that naturally occurs in a mound of pebbles. Then the room serves to evoke a sense memory for the clients, and every time they cross its threshold they're transported.

A few years ago I began using the ancient theory of the four elements as a discovery tool in my work. On a primal level, we need these elements to survive. The earth yields our food; fire gives us warmth; air and water sustain us. But since at least the era of the alchemical schools of ancient Egypt, various cultures have taken this concept a step further by designating the elements as the raw ingredients of the entire universe and basing their spiritual, mystical, magical, medical, philosophical, and scientific systems on them. The study of personality types goes back even further than the ancient dictum "know thyself," and it's most often associated with Hippocrates, who based his four humors or temperaments on the four elements. Carl Jung, one of the founders of modern psychology, linked the elements to the collective unconscious. In his version, fire corresponds to intuition, earth to sensation, air to thinking, and water to feeling. Buddhist teachings explain the elements in more sensory terms, perceiving water as fluid and cohesive; air as mobile and expansive; fire as passionate and energetic; and earth as stationary and solid. As spiritual, imaginative, and energetic templates, the elements are also principles of tarot and Western astrology and even the skeptics among us can have their moods lightened by reading a positive horoscope.

By nature, we all tend to gravitate to one element or another, and that preference taps into archetypal tastes and attitudes. It indicates how we perceive ourselves and our immediate world, and I've learned to interpret that leaning so it functions as a key to my clients' favorite colors, seasons, artwork, furniture, and fabrics. In broad terms, earth's grounding, steadfast energy is perfect for anywhere a family clusters—a media room, den, or kitchen. Water's energy purifies and cleanses, so it's conducive to tranquility, repose, and contemplation. Air energy clarifies and expands, so it's a great point of departure for a room dedicated to casual gatherings. Fire's transformative, vital energy matches high concentration and short-lived activities. One element may dominate a decor, or the elements may be equally blended, but in all cases the final design should feel cohesive.

Personally, I prefer to sleep in a water room, where curves and soft colors lull me into a state of relaxation. My dining rooms invariably feature fire, though, because fire stimulates people's opinions along with their taste buds. My living rooms generally have air as a strong influence, so that conversation circulates easily. A cozy space like a reading nook would revolve around the earth element.

This book divides several houses and apartments I recently designed according to their owners' proclivities for air, water, fire, or earth. Most spaces combine the elements in different proportions, and they all invariably contain some grounded earth energy. In general, an etheric balance of all four makes a space feel truly unique. So essentially I begin designing by looking through the lens of the four elements, and when an interior is finished I revisit it through the lens of a camera when I photograph it for publication. Once, that is, the clients assure me that they are truly in their element.

WATER

You must live in the present,
launch yourself on every wave,
find your eternity in each moment.

– Henry David Thoreau

In many cultures, a water feature—whether it is a fountain, a pond, or even a font—placed close to a front door is thought to energetically cleanse anyone who enters. And sure enough, every time I cross the moat surrounding one of my favorite hotels in Yangon, Burma, my stress simply evaporates. I've always seen water as therapeutic. I grew up in the Caribbean, so my affinity with the ocean started at an early age. These days, when I'm not traveling I spend my weekends in Montauk, where swimming and listening to the hypnotic sound of the tide clear my mind and refuel my creativity like nothing else. So the water-inspired spaces I design serve as restorative oases. Their main purpose is to wash away the cares of the day.

Vincent van Gogh and Édouard Manet used dreamy shades of green and blue to indicate water, and the palettes for my interiors are similarly impressionistic. A mercurial mix of silvery blues, grays, and pale greens symbolizes rivers and grassy banks. Then there's a range of beige and tan tones reminiscent of driftwood and seashells that can also recall wet sand, particularly if they're translated into a concrete floor. Buoyant soft whites, taupe, and pale celadon conjure up shores, sand dunes, and beach grasses. Pearlized cashmeres and faded pinks recall the inner surfaces of seashells, and independent of that they are universally flattering; women feel beautiful against them, and they don't intimidate men. Slate blue, charcoal gray, and black base tones also lend themselves to watery spaces, where they supply dynamic tension and reference deep seas and stormy rain clouds.

One reason we refer to water as a "body" is because it's able to split and then reconsolidate itself without losing its integrity. Some designers might convey that cohesiveness by employing only furnishings from a single period, but that's never been my style, and to my mind the uniformity of those types of interiors feels prescriptive and staccato. I always mix furniture and objects from different sources and eras, but for this element I make sure their structural essences embody some aspect of liquidity. As far as sinuous silhouettes go, Vladimir Kagan's Serpentine Sofa is quintessential, as are the benches Zaha Hadid based on cresting waves. The languid curves in Hans Wegner's Papa Bear Chair are intended to engulf the body; the sculptural lines in Isamu Noguchi's iconic coffee table and any of Charles Eames' bent plywood chairs rival river stones for their smooth, rounded edges, and Warren Platner's metal-rod tables have the energetic patterning of water jets. An ornate crystal chandelier reminds me of a frozen cascade that spouted icy prisms; Elsa Peretti's modernist candlesticks resemble a stream of molten silver, and Alvar Aalto's vases have the grace of a continuous ripple. Fabrics like marbleized cotton, silk damask, and anything with a lustrous sheen convey water's fluidity well, as do generously cut draperies that puddle into large folds on the floor.

Another of water's singularities is its need to recycle itself, so the smallest creek gets absorbed into a larger stream, then a lake or a river, until eventually it joins the sea or ocean. In architectural terms, this speaks to the hierarchy of spatial relationships, meaning that the size of a room correlates to its function and importance. It also speaks to building expectation and delaying gratification; it is, as Luis Barragán once put it, an "architectural striptease." It's an anteroom enclosing guests before the big reveal of entering a larger room. Or, to use the Taj Mahal as a more dramatic example, it's a tiny, dark doorway leading out to an expanse of garden, and at its very end is the payoff—the magnificent mausoleum!

Water's willingness to adopt and adapt to its container, be it a vase or a reservoir, makes it the most flexible of the elements. Its wide mutability range—from a teardrop to an icicle—qualifies it as a metaphor for change; chameleon-like, it can impersonate the other elements. As steam or vapor it's stabilized air; in its solid form, as ice, it bulks up and displays massing properties similar to those of earth. In interior design, this amounts to furniture layouts that aren't set in stone— arrangements that can casually change according to need. With that in mind, I keep things physically light here, as in my air spaces, and I go for anything that's multipurpose: a trestle table that expands to accommodate more guests; a stack of magazines doubling as an impromptu side table; an oversized ottoman that's additionally a seat and a coffee table surface. My clients tend to live informally, so I keep things loose, particularly when it comes to art, which I prefer to place rather than hang. I mount cantilevered picture ledges midway up one or more walls and lean or randomly overlap pictures and canvases. That's also how I handle my own photography collection in Manhattan. There, in true go-with-the-flow spirit, frames also rest against chair backs and sit on floors. Sometimes they're stacked two deep. To my mind, when a piece of art hangs in one place for a long time it comes to be taken for granted and its aesthetic value depreciates. No two waves curl identically, and no one is able to step into the same river twice, because movement is water's destiny. In interior design, this tendency plays out as a room's flow, its energetic path of entry and exit. A formal expression of this is an enfilade, where a series of on-axis doors link several aligned rooms. Another example would be any of the spatially layered houses that came out of the mid-twentieth-century modern architectural movement, where floating planes replaced traditional rooms and floor-to-ceiling window walls brought the outdoors inside. Then there are all the houses influenced by Frank Lloyd Wright, where living spaces circulate around a central core and mimic water's tendency to swirl concentrically. A consummate example of water architecture is the Fondation Louis Vuitton building on the outskirts of Paris, where Frank Gehry turned all things aquatic into a structural leitmotif. The museum he designed resembles a massive iceberg with a dozen glass sails, but because it sits in a sunken, flowing lake, it gracefully floats and rises from its own reflection. But the master of this type of building was Antoni Gaudí. His curved roofs resemble tidal swells; inside, halls merge and surge into stairwells, while walls stream into ceilings; random mosaics of glass and tile recall flotsam and jetsam. The flow inside my water-inspired spaces always feels intuitive. It meanders around furniture configurations; it passes by freestanding screens; it weaves close to a backlit panel. Water's reflective properties play a starring role in design. Ever since the tale was told of Narcissus, the son of a Greek river god who gazed into a pool and fell in love with himself, we've thought of mirrors as surreal portals into worlds where different realities collide. Take the Hall of Mirrors at Versailles, where hundreds of strategically placed mirrors animate arches and where arcaded windows bring in views of a magnificently sculpted garden. Somehow, the effect seems even grander on a smaller scale, as at my beach house, where mirrored stair risers trap ambulatory patches of sky from an adjacent window. I often lean large, framed mirrors when I need to open up a space or give it some symmetry; when I need to deflect light or project it into a dark corner; or when I'm aiming for some theatricality and illusion. These days I also like to hang immense sheets of polished steel. Their reflections are more beguiling and less literal than those of standard mirrors, but all types of shiny surfaces, from lacquer ware to glossy ceramic tiles, deserve to be around water.

If there's a foible in water's integration skills, it can be found in its inability to tolerate details. Imagine waves breaking on sand and dissolving footprints. Or there's Woody Allen's classic image of rain that "washes memories off the sidewalks of life." Water is all encompassing, and it favors large rather than small gestures, so I reserve intricately worked calligraphy or framed Persian miniatures for earth rooms, where they're better appreciated.

ABOUT WATER *According to Chinese philosophy, water is the most yin element, but when it's malevolent enough to fuel a raging sea it's clearly masculine. The ancient Greeks memorialized this element's femininity when they imagined Aphrodite, the ancient Greek goddess of love, rising from the sea, and that myth aligns with the fact that our blood and seawater have the same salinity. Water is a universal purifier, particularly when it falls as rain, which the book of Isaiah likens to the word of God — one nourishes the earth, while the other feeds the human soul. Baptism or any ceremonial anointment with water is believed to wipe the soul, or the psychic slate, clean.*

Water is essential to life — nothing survives or grows without it — and so its ritualistic use bestows blessings and acts as a conduit for devotion and prayer. The early Egyptians worshipped the Nile as a deity; pilgrims still perform their daily ablutions in the Ganges, while churchgoers reverentially dip their fingers into fonts. Dark, muddy water is mysterious and potentially frightening, while clear, odorless, colorless water represents all things chaste; white, frozen water has the proverbial purity of driven snow.

A single drop of water is anything but insignificant. To the Sufi poet Kahlil Gibran it contained all the secrets of all the oceans. Leonardo da Vinci imagined a droplet to be capable of raising the world's entire surface by an imperceptible amount, and over time a slowly dripping faucet can actually cleave a solid rock in two.

People with a water proclivity are grouped together under the astrological signs of Cancer, Scorpio, and Pisces, and they tend to be sociable and adventurous. In extreme they are unpredictable, especially when their reluctance to be pinned down is pronounced. Their emotional intensity may manifest as benevolence and compassion, in which case they make good caregivers. They're receptive to new ideas, but they are better interpreters than original thinkers. They're more comfortable dealing with the grand scheme than minutiae, and they'll develop multiple skills rather than master one. They tend to be self-motivated. Their instincts are sharp and they're often determined to find inner peace. It can be a challenge for them to overcome their fears, so they may be perceived as dark and mysterious. They believe in the subconscious, dream analysis, mysticism, and romance, and they're often prone to nostalgia. They frequently have physical grace, but a person with an excess of water traits can get maudlin, depressed, or even addicted when ungrounded or lacking sufficient earth. I liken that to a water room painted in ethereal colors that's in need of a solid, stabilizing anchor, such as a chair or a table constructed from slate or marble or grainy wood.

FIRE

Fire's ferocity complements the serenity of the air and water spaces for which I'm best known. Unlike earth, air, and water, fire is much more than a mere material. It's a raw phenomenon, a self-perpetuating chemical reaction that thrives on extremes. In an interview, I once described myself as "a combination of sarcastic and sweet, funny and deadpan, hard-working and escapist, political and unconscious, politically incorrect and concerned, all mixed into a Latino interior and covered in a shell of New York sophistication." Well, fire is just as dichotomous. Energetically it's both joyful and destructive. It has an instinctive urge to kiss and to annihilate, to be angelic and demonic. Its diversity qualifies it as the most revered and feared of the elements, and I'm always up for the challenges and complexities it poses in interiors.

Light affects design more than any other component, and two sun-drenched rooms illustrate what I mean about fire's dual personality. In one, filtered incoming light bathes all the furnishings in a nostalgic, golden glow; in the second, where the light is unfiltered, it pours in relentlessly and eventually leaches out all the textile and surface colors. Photographing an interior is similar. Too much direct light obliterates all the nuances, but too little shrouds everything in gloom. So handling fire requires an even hand.

Fierce shades of red are stereotypically associated with fire, but I dip into the color's entire repertoire—from coral to crimson, ruby to rust, magenta to mahogany—whenever an interior needs a shot of adrenalin. Painters have taught me a lot about using red judiciously. J.M.W. Turner used a dab of it to symbolize hope in a stormy sea; Auguste Renoir likened a brushstroke of it to a sonorous bell; Henri Matisse considered a thimbleful of it to be more effusive than a bucketful. I cook a lot, and just as I recognize the potency of a dash of hot sauce, I know that one fiery gesture is often all that's needed to spice up an interior. An armchair upholstered in plum leather, a cinnabar box, a copper-lined fireplace, a hot pink rug against brown walls—each one acts like a dose of cayenne. Or, to give a fashion parallel, a curtain's magenta backing enlivens a sedate decor the way a woman's conservative cocktail attire gets its panache from the red soles of her Christian Louboutin high heels.

But I don't define fire strictly according to pigment. I define it as intensity. Fire is any pronounced or concentrated color or material. Mark Rothko's abstracts epitomize that. Even when his paintings are black, they project an inner radiance and a spectrum of moods, from ecstatic to tragic. Edgar Degas qualifies, too, for his amazing range of blacks and browns mixed with soft greens and yellows. Then there are Edward Weston's fiery black-and-white photographs of dunes that I would classify in the earth category if they weren't so spirited and tonally rich. I rank much of Frida Kahlo and Francis Bacon's work as fiery for their use of color but also for the audaciousness of the subject matter.

In a reserved, neutral interior fire, could even be one rococo chair. It's any dynamic presence that tips the aesthetic scales into resolution. I was once sitting in a client's bright white living room when he started reminiscing about Bali, so we decided to pepper in some fuchsia and orange pillows. Another time we animated a bathroom by painting it a deep turquoise; a deep sienna finish we once applied to a foyer amplified its hospitality.

One fiery accent stops us in our tracks, but whenever red or any strong color floods an entire room it has the opposite effect. When red covers a large interior, it becomes a magnetic draw. My commercial clients love the theatricality of a monochrome red restaurant, particularly when the cuisine being served is piquant. The surroundings validate the food the way Luis Barragán's colors blaze in the hot Mexican sun. Studies show evidence that red elevates blood pressure and respiratory rates, which may be why it's a staple in casinos. I base the allure of my monochrome palettes on a range of several similar tones. In a living room I once designed for a showhouse, I let six red shades from oxblood to orange mingle with each other, and the end result was as seductive as it was peaceful.

Fire rooms works best when they're flanked by earth, air, and water spaces. They serve as cocoons and ignite contrast. But when two fire spaces lead into each other, their drama gets diluted. The amount of fire I invest in a room depends on the activity that takes place there. I recently lined a library's walls with burgundy metallic leather because the client likes to spend bursts of time with his vast collection of art books. Fire also works well in dining rooms, where it provides the spark for mere dinners to evolve into dinner parties.

In the mid-1950s, Billy Baldwin designed one of the most frequently published fire rooms of all time. The eminently stylish editor Diana Vreeland asked him for "a garden in hell," and he obliged by covering her living room with scarlet chintz. Vreeland thought of red as a revealing clarifier, a catalyst that enhanced all other colors, but she defined her shade categorically as "rococo with a spot of Gothic in it and a bit of Buddhist temple." Most of us are specific when it comes to our favorite reds. For example, I prefer mine with a splash of orange, not blue. Ironically, if Baldwin had hewed more closely to the traditional version of hell, Vreeland's room might have ended up looking ghostly, because when fire rages, as it supposedly does in hell, its blue, indigo, and violet body turns hot white. It's fascinating to think of fire and snow as the same color! Even a mild blaze isn't consistently red—it fluctuates between orange, green, and yellow. Even candles burn bluish at their bases and yellow at their tips.

Fire and light are synonymous. Both glow, and in the hands of an interior designer both convey emotion. In general, fire calls for dramatic lighting. I usually mix standing, ceiling, and table fixtures. I use sconces whenever a wall needs some jewelry; black metal ceiling pendants with beaten copper interiors resemble overturned cauldrons and work well in tight, intimate spaces. A Sputnik chandelier with a dozen spiny arms resembles a starburst firework and needs to hang low with nothing around it. In most spiritual traditions, one lit candle is a vehicle for prayer—its singularity has significance—but the flames from a cluster of candles generate the most beneficent, flattering, forgiving light, hiding flaws, saturating colors, and softening angles.

Just as a chimney affects the pitch of a roof, a fireplace and its surround are usually a room's largest focal point. They establish the hierarchal placement of furniture, but other things can provide that same kind of nucleus: a Chinese lacquered cabinet, a sofa upholstered in maroon mohair, a hand-painted console. In a showhouse room I once took things literally and used a videotape loop of Mount Vesuvius as my fire component. By the way, I never hide television screens. They flicker just like hearths. One could make the argument that bedrooms also qualify as fiery, because they're linked to passion, but I prefer my clients to retire to tranquil water spaces framed around cool, diffused taupes, off-whites, and pale blues.

Just as several scattered fires quickly die down, several dispersed fire components feel apathetic. Design gestures are more effective en masse. Think of a group of mauve cushions strewn across a taupe sofa; five stacks of books on a coffee table rather than one; two or three bunches of long-stemmed, Schiaparelli pink tulips in a vase. As the tale of Icarus flying too close to the sun illustrates, a real-life fire is best observed from a distance. But as far as decor is concerned, a fiery room can be just as mesmerizing as the real thing, and it doesn't scorch.

The fire element is considered to be masculine or yang, and its association with fame and pure genius is brilliantly illustrated in a gemstone's luster or a diamond's resplendence. In the Bible, fire is the light striving to overcome darkness while it's also the fabric of hell. God is often described as "a consuming fire," and in some beliefs spiritual enlightenment is attained through an individual's inner fire.

According to the ancient Greeks, Prometheus stole fire from the gods and gave it to humans, but in many cultures' myths, fire was introduced by an animal — a coyote, wolf, woodpecker, monkey, ostrich, hummingbird, fox, or jaguar. But as man is indisputably the only species able to control fire, and oxygenated earth has the only known atmosphere capable of hosting it, fire exemplifies human superiority.

Red entrances have always been strongly symbolic, whether representing status, superiority, high visibility, or hospitality. A palace's red gates instilled fear in the people of ancient China, and to this day a red door is believed to ward off evil in some parts of the world, while in other parts it deters traveling salespeople, invites good fortune, or simply protects whoever crosses its threshold. In an ashram, a red wall prompts aspirants to stay mindful, and all-red rooms have a particular resonance from the nightmarish chamber of Jane Eyre's childhood to Henri Matisse's seminal L'Atelier Rouge (The Red Studio), a painting that reevaluated perspective at the beginning of the twentieth century.

People with a preponderance of fire energy are seen as determined, passionate, and willful. Governed by the astrological signs of Leo, Aries, and Sagittarius, they're often classified as spirits in motion. Charismatic leaders who can light up a room as soon as they enter, they have an enviable lust for life and often have air-oriented people at their sides encouraging them. They're radiant and warm, spontaneous and playful, and their intuition leads them to search for new experiences. They like to live large and often feel frustrated by mundane chores and duties. They rely on instinct, although they often skip crucial steps, and they're oblivious to the effect they have on other people. Someone who is "on fire" has harnessed the muse or is in the midst of an inspired phase, but someone with excessive fire can be gluttonous, volatile, obsessive, and hot-headed. In design, a fiery addition to an interior always makes a statement. It's often the unexpected, unpredictable component that unites everything and makes a room sing. It often qualifies as a "wow factor," or it's a fulcrum that I sometimes refer to as harmonious tension because it gives a decor some needed edge and jolts it out of its complacency.

AIR

There's an atmospheric similarity between a successful air room and a slice of azure sky. They're both expansive, calming, and ethereal; both as uplifting as Frank Sinatra's version of "Come Fly with Me." Human nature tends to mirror outer nature, and the state of mind we most often express in celestial terms is elation. We're "starry eyed," "over the moon," or "in seventh heaven." Even when photographers like Alfred Stieglitz and painters including Titian and Vincent van Gogh projected tempestuous moods onto billowy clouds, they still saw the skies as a source of nourishment, as the "daily bread of our eyes," as Ralph Waldo Emerson deemed it. Constellations orient us; clouds act like weathervanes and the sun delineates time. In one of Henri Cartier-Bresson's iconic photographs, a woman praying on a hilltop in Srinagar tilts her head upwards, her arms outstretched, as she communes with the sky, which in turn seems to send her spiritual sustenance. In a contemporary installation—a windowless, four-sided structure with no ceiling—the artist James Turrell actually lets people bathe in the sky's immensity. All of these things come to mind when I design an air room.

When an apartment or house feels spacious, that's generally due to its proportions or, in the words of Edith Wharton, its architectural "good breeding." For example, two kitchens may have the same width and length, but if one has a taller ceiling it seems airier. Through practice, most interior designers also become illusionists. We know how to compensate for a lack of height or square footage, and although I don't go around slicing the lids off of my projects, as Turrell does, I often use silver leaf to elevate a ceiling visually. More often than not, color and texture are the only tools I need to stretch or foreshorten any structural surface, and whenever I envelop an entire space in white or gray its horizons open wide. Air is omnipresent: it doesn't start or stop anywhere, so it blurs boundaries and amplifies space. Treating a whole room or home with a gradual sequence of sympathetic tones has a similar effect, as does removing doorframes, baseboards, and any other superfluous molding, allowing the eye to travel across an interior landscape in one even sweep.

The master of integration, white is prominent in my air schemes because it creates a continuum by uniting different styles and shapes. A white background also happens to be a wonderful foil. It flatters everyone, no matter their age or complexion. I favor crisp whites with the least possible dilution of another pigment and find them to be impartial and pure, neither cool nor warm, like the range I created for PPG Pittsburgh Paints. The majority of colors I use are receptive to the quality and density of surrounding light, so they intensify or recede according to the sun's position. Overuse of vivid white can rob a space of its humanity. Such a space can come across as icy and harsh, but in moderation white can be mesmerizing and transporting. In my Montauk house, every time I leave my bedroom and walk into my remarkably white bathroom, I enter another dimension. Muted taupes and stone colors animate white by amplifying its brightness with their gentle and whispery tonality. Air is also attracted to buoyant, buttery yellows and pearl grays with an undertone of pink. It also likes bluish lavenders and powder blues, so long as they're spiked with a dose of black to cut their sweetness and prevent them from dissipating.

Light figures prominently in air interiors, and any openings to the outside not only let in fresh air and sun, but also eliminate any notion of confinement. A cross-breeze in a tiny log cabin brings in the smell of newly mown grass; an open French door leads the eye to a porch or verandah; a skylight joins our vision to our imagination and lets them both soar. Undressed windows suit air rooms, unless privacy is an issue, in which case I hang curtains from barely visible tension wire and install roman shades that all but disappear into the header when they're folded up. By placing a light behind a wall—especially if the wall is freestanding and doesn't meet the ceiling—I can create an assumption of space and in the bargain I get a glowing perimeter halo. Whenever I float a piece of artwork in front of a bank of sheer or solid curtains that I've lit from behind, I create visual depth, and the whole vignette practically levitates. All these things add up to a dreamlike, surreal ambience.

My air spaces are gravity-defying zones, so none of the furniture or accessories come across as heavy, affixed, or immovable. Arrangements should appear uncontrived, as if the pieces glided into just the right spot. There are any number of sturdy, featherweight chairs on the market—Gio Ponti's classic Superleggera Chair and Marcel Wanders' Knotted Chair with a carbon seat come to mind—but I'm more concerned with visual weightlessness. So I focus on how things resolve themselves on the floor. Shapely or translucent legs have a particular grace and agility, as does a sofa mounted on a recessed base.

An air space has the same harmonic tension between materials that crops up throughout my work, but here it's more of an aesthetic dance. It's the sweet spot between opposites: diaphanous fabrics against hard surfaces; rough textures against smooth and shiny; angular shapes alongside curves. And there's a play on scale, so a tall, stately silhouette likely sits adjacent to something short and plump, to play around with our perceptions of space.

Air interacts well with transparent solid materials that seriously throw off our preconceptions about perspective. The glass, clear Lucite, and resin I use for tables, chairs, and partitions have substance but no visual heft. Eero Saarinen's Ball Chair is one of my favorite designs, especially when it's hung from a ceiling so it appears to take up no space whatsoever. Lit from within, the semi-translucent, white resin cubes I use as end tables resemble drifting banks of fog. Air's flighty personality perfectly suits gauzy, diaphanous fabrics that layer and veil vistas; they undulate in an incoming breeze or endlessly ripple in the path of a whirring fan. Suede, velvet, fur, and shaggy silk rugs are sympathetic to air, and any indentations in their nap and pile might be the signature left by a gust of wind. The finish on a strié wall, where glaze applied on top of a base coat is then troweled with a brush, looks as if it could be windswept sand.

As far as editing goes, I eliminate up to the point just before minimalism. I'm spare but never austere. I always ask myself, "Do I love this object? Does it speak to me in a clear voice? Is it a visual necessity?" And if the answer isn't a resounding yes or no—if I have to qualify it for any reason—experience tells me that I don't need it. The term "negative space"—where form teams up with non-form—is a misnomer because it's beneficial to give every object a respectful amount of air. The Japanese aesthetic principle of ma sees air as a vital component of any composition and refers to spatial noiselessness. In music, this type of silence qualifies as a rest,and in prose and poetry it's a lacuna or a caesura, but all cases acknowledge the importanceof nothing. When it's framed by air an object comes into its own and is given permission to breathe. Its uniqueness shines much like a photographic portrait where the subject is shot against a white seamless background without any props. Isolating an object by mounting it on a stand or plinth has an even stronger effect and once there's a perfect balance of air, possibilities emerge and, well, the sky's the limit!

ABOUT AIR *The sun rises in the east, which is also air's principal direction, so anything that dawns—a day, a new age, an idea—symbolically connects to this element. If, as some scientists believe, human atoms originated billions of years ago in exploding stars, then the sky is our place of origin and air is the first principle of life. Even though our lungs can accommodate up to two gallons of air, most of us settle for two to three pints. In one of several ancient air myths, the Greek goddess Athena breathes life into man moments before he is defined as human. In another, primal wind fertilizes itself, transforms into desire, and separates earth, water, and fire from each another. In another, the Egyptian sky goddess, Nut, is depicted naked and covered with stars as her fingers and toes touch the four cardinal points.*

In most spiritual beliefs, air bridges the lower and higher realms of existence, and in practices like yoga and meditation, intentional breathing—nothing if not the control of air—energetically connects the soul, mind, and body. Atmospherically, air allows us to hear, visualize, and in the form of an exhalation produces vibration, tone, words, and song. Air alone is the substance of sound. We regularly refer to air as "fresh" when, in fact, its recirculated particles have existed since time immemorial and therefore link us to every plant or sentient being that ever was or will be. People who are drawn to air are typically curious and cooperative. They have an innate sense of perspective; they multi-task well and appreciate diversity. They are abstract thinkers and they tend to comprehend the big picture. Grouped under the astrological signs of Libra, Aquarius, and Gemini, they are born conversationalists, which is why air rooms make perfect stages for social gatherings. Air types don't particularly value tradition. They are attracted to innovation and may choose to experiment with alternative lifestyles, so their homes, studios and offices are unlikely to be populated with antiques or memorabilia. They tend to relish the future more than the past, so they are rarely impressed by an object's provenance. They also are not overly concerned with tidiness, or they need to keep their belongings in some kind of systemized order. They may employ unique filing methods that only they can decipher. Though they're often charming, they live life by their own rules, so they sometimes lack social graces. An excess of air may make a person seem pretentious or aloof, absentminded or impractical. In all cases, air needs a dose of earth energy to bring it back to reality, and in design that translates into any material that's organic, textured, or patinated.

EARTH

Earth laughs
in flowers.

– Ralph Waldo Emerson

When I design an earth space, I think about my client's definition of home as well as all the different configurations of nesting. My lyrical version of an earth space is a clearing in a forest where light glimmers through the trees and dapples beds of warm moss. But in purely practical terms, this element is all about safe havens, stress-free inner sanctums, and a pervasive sense of security. Chinese cosmology describes earth energy as inwardly oriented and balanced, and in my work that translates to a man cave, private study, sitting room, bedroom, media room, or any other place where a client is likely to hibernate or hole up for long periods of time. Earth walls need to feel sturdy and substantial, so I line them with grass cloth or other textured material, or if there's existing wainscoting I'll emphasize it. In libraries, I often install floor-to-ceiling wood paneling, channeling elegant, substantial Parisian boiserie. Comfort is also central to earth, so I bring in cashmere throws, lots of cushions, broad bergères with generous, down-filled pillows, and deep-seated sofas and ottomans that promote relaxation and encourage informality. The embracing shape offered by an Arne Jacobsen Egg chair and contemporary wingbacks epitomizes refuge, and the only real way to appreciate the sensuous curves in Eero Saarinen's Womb chair is to curl up in it and lean back. I've traveled extensively throughout Asia where reclining is the norm, so I love chaises and I look on antique four-poster Chinese beds as sheltering cabins in their own right. When I float one in the center of a large space, it's a surefire invitation for people to kick off their shoes, climb in, and totally unwind.

Just as seeds flourish in fertile soil, ideas germinate and come to fruition in fleshed-out earth rooms, as they are well-suited to creativity. Pets and plants thrive in these spaces, and they're ideal stages for voluptuous vases of flowers whose colors coordinate with the season, although harvest yellows and golds reverberate at any time of the year. Pale and lime greens summon up spring; rust, orange, and burgundy typify fall; primary colors and rich, emerald greens celebrate summer. In my experience, people with astrological earth signs are inclined to be acquisitive, and their appreciation for beauty ranges widely, so I invariably need to accommodate their large book collections with walls of shelves. When it comes to art, my preference is for large-scale pieces that lend stature. An iconic example would be a robust bronze by Auguste Rodin or Henry Moore. Classic earth images include Georgia O'Keeffe's paintings of cottonwood trees and desert flowers from her New Mexico period and photographer Lynn Davis's monolithic stones or marble quarries. Jean Michel-Basquiat's canvases can work with any element, but to my mind his raw technique and his drive to explore his origins are very earthy.

This element needs a solid base, so floor treatments are key. In main entries I sometimes make up a pattern of squares and circles out of wood and stone so guests immediately know they've landed. Rectangular antique oushaks or faded Persian rugs are my first choices for covering living room floors, where their traditional floral motifs bring to mind fruitful meadows. Lime-rubbed or hewn oak, as well as ebony or dark mahogany-stained planks with pronounced grain, come across as terra firma. Vegetable-dyed kilims and thick sisal runners laid over driftwood boards convey a natural dynamism. Circular rugs accommodate all shapes of furniture, and their unity is grounding, perhaps because their shape echoes the planet's? Animals in all forms and representations epitomize earth, whether in the form of a cowhide that replaces a conventional rug, a lamb's wool-upholstered stool, a shagreen box, or an animal skull. In one way an earth room's ceiling functions as its sky, and I prefer white finishes that optically add height and reflect incoming light. In cases where there's harsh light, I either cover windows with minimal shades that also soften the architecture or I hang glazed wool draperies—with full-bodied folds and ample hems—to direct the gaze inward.

Earth buildings allude to the land in obvious ways. An earth building may have a thriving garden, a green roof, or a vertical wall of vegetation. Others are structurally integrated into their sites, like Frank Lloyd Wright's Fallingwater. Some utilize organic materials, such as straw bale, bamboo, rammed earth, adobe, cordwood, or stone. All of these external materials weather organically and complement the interior materials with the wabi-sabi appeal of imperfection. Wood shows signs of aging; stainless steel counters accumulate scratches; rust and tarnish qualify as patina. Seminal pieces of furniture include a well-worn 1930s leather armchair picked up at the Clignancourt flea market in Paris or an Indonesian carved chair with an uneven pearl inlay. Signs of the maker's hand are also desirable: a mouth-blown glass vase; an eighteenth-century suzani with slightly irregular chain stitching.

I supply the majority of accessories in my projects, but I customize them based on my clients' tastes and lifestyles, and I enjoy finding them on my travels. For this element, I think of things like a teak mask picked up on a trip to Nairobi; a large quartz crystal brought back from Brazil; an embroidered Asian textile that started life as part of a dowry; a Chinese rosewood yoke-back chair from an era when the simple act of sitting denoted rank; an Ashanti stool carved out of a single block of wood; a hammered brass door that once fronted an eighteenth-century Indian haveli; overscale architectural finials; enameled snuffboxes inlaid with mother-of-pearl; Indonesian serving spoons carved out of horn or a collection of Tibetan dorjes. I also pick up stones or bird feathers when I'm away to remind myself of colors, but I never duplicate them exactly. Back in my studio I adjust their tones once I've put them into context and figured in my client's sensibility. The word "humble" stems from the Latin *humus* meaning earth, and that linguistic connection reminds me never to treat rare, one-of-a-kind, or museum-quality objects as if they're overly precious or untouchable. They're best integrated throughout a project in places where they can be handled and admired close up. Across the board, I rarely go for ornamentation. I feel it's most often used to express agitation and not decorative grace. But when I do, one piece—like an ornate, Chinese paneled bed—suffices. I admire designers like Tony Duquette who layered pattern on texture, and Pauline de Rothschild's apartments have always inspired me with their balance of fantasy and reality. There's a living room where she used antique floral wallpaper flush with a surrounding wall to conceal a jib door—the most stylish hideaway. But I crave the clarity that comes when a strong statement is made with less rather than more. I love adornment when it's intrinsic to a raw material, which is why I'm a fan of George Nakashima, whose furniture respects wood as if it were a tree's soul.

Earth rooms are a balance of yin and yang, so they appeal to both sexes. That's actually true of all of my work because opposites—rough and smooth; dark and light; small and large—produce a harmonious tension. So for this element, a sofa has plump feather pillows, but its skirt has tailored pleats. A textured linen wall covering balances smoothly lacquered woodwork. A dining table's gnarled wood top is offset by a satin nickel base. A silken carpet overlaps rough stone floors, and nubby chenille upholstery is strewn with shiny pillows. My colors are also gender neutral. For example I would never use baby pink in a clichéd way, but I might use it in the form of a piece of broadloom, laid at an angle underneath a master bed to define space, just like any other architectural gesture.

ABOUT EARTH *Water flows, air rises, fire leaps, but earth stays put. It's the ground beneath our feet that also allows itself to be graded and piled into mountains, which is why Vastu shastra, the ancient Hindu science of architecture, ranks it as the most important element. Early Roman philosophers designated earth as the origin of all material things, as did the Bible, where Adam is the masculine form of a word meaning "earth" and Eve means "source of life." This element is both benevolent and ruthless, because it eventually consumes its bounty. Barbaric or not, earth ranks as the only self-sustaining planet and is exemplified by the energetic marriage of yin and yang, with its black and white symbol. Despite the earth's masculine/feminine balance, it is often alluded to as a mother. Indeed, in Greek mythology goddesses outnumber gods, and Gaia, the Greek earth goddess, created herself out of primordial chaos. In several ancient creation stories a creature of no particular gender — in Japan, a gigantic fish; in India, a tortoise; in Egypt, a scarab; in South America, a serpent; in Southeast Asia, an elephant — holds up the earth and whenever it walks or rotates its head it sets off a quake, a tremor, or some other natural disaster. To the Mayans the earth was one flat surface with each of its four corners pointing in a cardinal direction. Lunar eclipses taught the ancient Greeks to see the planet as a globe, and Magellan circumnavigated that globe in the sixteenth century, but remarkably the International Flat Earth Research Society still boasts an active membership. Ruled by the astrological signs of Taurus, Virgo, and Capricorn, earth people are homebodies who lap up comfort and flourish when they perceive their surroundings as literally or visually luxurious. They enjoy the tactile side of material things and are arguably more in tune with the five senses — hearing, sight, smell, taste, and touch — than other types. They tend to be acquisitive, and their happiness, fulfillment, and level of well-being tend to increase when they are settled and surrounded by their things. The Tarot suit of Pentacles, which represents earth, connects to the five senses. In extreme cases, earth people can become hoarders who amass stuff indiscriminately and have fears about detaching from their possessions; in elevated, sophisticated form, that tendency can produce a curator. People with a predominance of earth invariably rank as solid, longtime friends — "bricks," to use an informal British term. They're genuine, balanced, reliable, helpful, no-nonsense, and pragmatic — literally "down to earth." They think in the long term, so they are community minded and often environmentally aware. Rather than intuitive or impulsive, they are methodical. They accumulate knowledge from hands-on experience and their preference for learning by doing endows them with patience and holistic comprehension. Too little earth can render someone impractical, unrealistic, and ungrateful, but an excess of earth may turn someone into an overt sensualist or, conversely, a "stick in the mud" who values routine over spontaneity.*

APPENDIX

Select images below are captioned with the specific paint colors that I was inspired by in designing the rooms.

All paints by PPG Pittsburgh Paints.

All four elements — earthy Tanzanian masks; sconces that cast fiery light upward; an abstract oil of a gushing waterfall; and a console's airy outline — balance a foyer.

In my Montauk hallway, lacquered surfaces capture watery, garden reflections, and Mr. Mischa prances across Crab Orchard stone floors as warm light touches an eighteenth-century Thai Buddha.

Purifying, deep, reflective, clarifying, ever-changing — several of the words I associate with the water element are epitomized in this image I shot of a lake in Vietnam.

Early morning mists and light fog rising from Ha Long Bay in Vietnam remind me of water's transformative properties and its affinity with both earth and air.

In an airy, high-rise living room, nineteenth-century chairs upholstered in dark camel leather stabilize an aqua color scheme and a reflective glass table — classic water features.

Water's adaptability inspired me to use liquid gray-blues in a home office that effortlessly transforms into a spare bedroom as needed.

Mirrors — surrounding a grid of upholstered panels, left, and a Damien Hirst painting, right — expand the energy in two entries and offset their earthier aspects.

Upholstery colors inspired by views of the ocean help unite a master bedroom and its adjoining sitting room in a Hamptons beach house.

A silver-leaf niche wall behind a headboard provides a dreamy, diffuse layer in a romantic bedroom that sits, aerie-like, above Manhattan.

In a dining room, containers — 1920s vases bordering the walls and a line-up of enamel pitchers — serve as literal references to the water element.

Silver Blueberry 1163-5

A Japanese kimono stand, left, and a Chinese ladder, right, function as towel racks and symbolize the unity of sky and earth, balancing the overt water aspects of two bathrooms.

Fond Memory 527-4   Gray Beard 540-2

A client who has an astrological water sign asked me to use as much blue as possible — in the upholstery, carpet, and marble-topped coffee table — in a den connected to her kitchen.

Water unifies and assimilates objects from India, Mali, France, and Latin America, left. A cube light, right, acts as a monumental yet ethereal segue onto Manhattan's skyline whenever it is illuminated.

Blue Dolphin 549-4   Quicksilver 549-5   Seagull 520-3

Purple Dragon 1247-4   Real Simple 1096-4   Thin Ice 518-3

Swivel chairs and a spectrum of deep blues bring fluidity to a sitting room centered around a leather ottoman/coffee table.

Shapely Verner Panton chairs illustrate water's flexibility and adaptability; opposite is a dining banquette flanked by wooden armchairs.

An eighteen-foot pitch to the ceiling and ethereal colors underscore the pleasantly adrift feel of a Connecticut bedroom. A gilded home shrine from China lends an affirming touch of fire.

In a Hamptons living room, silvery, translucent curtains mimic sunlight streaking across waves, while a reflective wall of stainless steel references the ocean's expansiveness.

Whether inside or outdoors, water decor craves focus and structure, as in a massive lampshade, left, and, right, a cabana at the end of a swimming pool.

Suggestions of water ripple throughout a bathroom — from the frosted glass island countertop to the back-to-back sinks, floating mirror, and glass-enclosed shower.

Pageant Song 1163-3   Pink Chintz 138-4

A bedroom's overt dreaminess — tranquil colors, an upholstered wall, gauze-covered windows — is brought down to earth with asymmetrical lamps and mismatched side tables.

The palette of a Hamptons living room connects to the nearby beach, ocean, and sky. Imaginary flotsam and jetsam inspired the placement of disparate furnishings.

Chalky Blue 552-5   Coast of Maine 10-20   Rock Cliffs 1101-4

Tinsel 555-3

A primitive country cabinet with straight lines appears modern when juxtaposed against simple drapes and sliding glass doors in my Montauk beach house.

In my Montauk house, a Louise Dahl-Wolfe photograph displayed on a table has the horizon line as a backdrop. In a bedroom, a refectory table directs the eye toward the water view.

A Chinese bed floats on a raft-like piece of white glass that is set into a sand-blasted wood floor, while a lacquered ceiling and steel-paneled wall amplify the ocean's expansiveness.

A sparse, dramatic savanna shot at sunset in Tanzania represents how I apply the fire element in my interior design – sparingly, to highlight its vitality.

I took this shot of a blazing pink sky at sunset as we were leaving the vibrant city of Isfahan, south of Tehran, and it still reminds me of the relationship between fire and air.

Ancient Copper 1063-7

A Manhattan living room comes into its own in the evening whenever the glow cast by candlelight mixes with reflective light from an Achille Castiglioni table lamp and the city's lights.

Fire elements up the ante in neutral spaces. Left, saffron pillows and a tangerine Warren Platner chair; right, a shapely Chinese chair and an ornate nineteenth-century mirror frame.

In a Kips Bay show house den and TV room, orange-red walls counteract the blandness of generic paneling. I selected the same unifying accent shade for soft and hard materials.

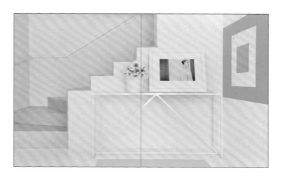

Pairing opposites creates harmonious friction. Left, textural rusticity and refinement. Right, Damien Hirst artwork as a repository of energy in a predominantly neutral vignette.

Firelight 1211-5   Pollination 1215-7

A coral-colored wall, bed linens, and window shades energize a small guest bedroom in Florida. The saturated green Burmese table relates to a view of palm trees outside.

Geometric planes of applied color surrounding the bright white, stepped wall of an angular staircase all play with different levels of hue intensity in this entrance hall.

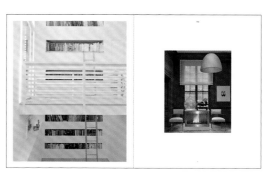

Organizing book spines by color, left, brings zest to a rigorous, cerebral entrance. A freestanding fireplace, right, slows the pace and transforms an area into a hearth.

In a masculine home office in Westchester, light seeping through wooden Venetian blinds exaggerates the grainy texture of mahogany wall panels.

Reflective surfaces and ornately carved candlesticks, left, introduce the fire element subtly; a Sputnik lamp and animal print and blue sateen upholstery, right, introduce it dramatically.

Chinese Porcelain 1160-6

Earth's fiery aspects are showcased in the terra-cotta artifacts that dot a dining room where spirited discussions take place around two slate tables on wheels.

The sconces and Sputnik pendant in this dining room are on dimmer switches so their light doesn't upstage the gilt detailing on the cinnabar Chinese cabinets that flank the fireplace.

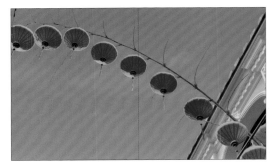

Feathery light, paper-thin Chinese lanterns strung high across a street in Laos convey air's tendency to expand space. They also give the illusion of weightlessness.

At the twelfth-century Angkor Wat temple in Cambodia, shadow play from a strong source of western light injects a suggestion of weightlessness into an imposing sandstone corridor.

Discover 1021-3   Elusion 1005-2

A pair of sculptural Dogon ladders soar upward alongside a winding staircase in a Westchester foyer.

A receding white wall and lounger, left, are absorbed into the negative space around this painting. A horizontal mirror, right, injects volume and airiness into a small foyer.

Angling the carpet and table allows a wide foyer to double as a dining space. Billowy curtains beckon guests to venture outside into a manicured garden.

California Wine 1184-7   Fall Leaf 1197-6   Wet Coral 1189-6

A bookcase hides a door that's affixed to a recessed ceiling track. When it is closed it provides privacy for a bedroom; when open, the space enjoys cross-breezes.

Sky colors visible from a sitting room adjacent to a bedroom, left, echo in its blue-gray walls. A rolling steel table, right, brings flexibility to a living room's seating area.

Ways to insert light and air — a backlit steel tray suspended above a dining table accentuates the height of the coffered ceiling, while a leaning mirror magnifies the illusion.

Bookshelves recessed into mirrored alcoves and a fireplace with a reflective surround visually widen and extend the perceived square footage of a media room.

With no carpet to interrupt the flow, an abundance of light and air allows the eye to travel through windows and the adjacent rooms, and perceive this Westchester entryway as endless.

Smooth, shapely objects alongside crisp white upholstery and pastel flowers complement this graphic framed Fernand Léger and encourage it to breathe.

Light filtering through glazed ceramic screens creates the impression of continued space behind a hallway, left, and, a kitchen banquette, right.

A limited palette of ethereal grays unifies two seating areas in a Manhattan loft, encouraging a circulatory flow and an energetic exchange.

Applesauce Cake 1095-5   Eagle Eye 1014-6

Gray Shadows 1005-3

In a penthouse living room, windows and incoming light define the seating sections and blue and white upholstery colors feel akin to sky views.

In a Hamptons living room, an army of white pottery floats on open shelving near extended views through oversized windows and French doors.

Spice Is Nice 1090-2

From a cabriole-leg table to a deeply curved sofa, a living room's shapely furniture floats away from its walls and spotlights an airy yellow canvas.

A skylight, a mirror, and lacquered surfaces amplify the airiness of a bathroom, while a dark wood sink surround and a wall-mounted fireplace save it from visually floating away.

A snug corner banquette feels anything but confined thanks to the way schoolhouse and standard shades modulate rooftop and sky views on Madison Avenue.

A collection of unframed, rectilinear art hung salon-style in a Tel Aviv house appears to defy gravity as it plays up the open clarity of the foyer's perfect proportions.

American Anthem 1156-4

Thick black frames on a floor-to-ceiling collection of Robert Longo watercolors serve as an architectural intervention and visually deepen and extend one wall of a kitchen.

Both an undulating wall paired with a wingback chair, left, and a bronze Diego Giacometti console with bowed legs, right, simulate the rippling effect of air.

A circular ottoman placed centrally beneath the octagonal ceiling of a Hamptons pool/card room stands in the center of a set of mismatched chairs.

Floating a console in front of a window and surrounding it with furniture of various heights and proportions means the eye is never stationary, and as it journeys it perceives more space.

A vintage Lucite side chair and a cantilevered wall-to-wall sofa with no detectable means of support both help to expand a cozy media room spatially.

A low screen defines a Palm Beach apartment's foyer without restricting the flow of sunlight that streams into the living and dining areas beyond.

Light clarifies a layered furniture plan and makes it comprehensible. It delineates seating areas, left, and separates a Chinese octagonal table from a grand piano and a staircase, right.

Canyon Peach 1070-1   Stargazer 1011-3

A stone floor in a Montauk dining room conjures up the colors and textures of the neighboring beach, while the lacquered ceiling reflects an adjacent garden.

Violet Vogue 1249-1

A deliberate sequence of white – in a Louise Nelson sculpture, a banquette, and leather upholstered armchairs – infuses a dining room with air.

Ample amounts of northern light complement a wide range of materials – gilt wood, cowhide, stainless steel – and make a family out of furniture sourced from different countries.

A wall-to-wall dining banquette visually widens a dining room where morning light bounces across the room after it's reflected in an oversized wall mirror.

A freestanding tub, a mirrored vanity and stool, and a leaning Chinese ladder allow unobstructed light in a Westchester bathroom.

Fourteen-foot-high sheer curtains provide privacy in this Westchester family room yet let in fresh air and vistas; dark, visually weighty furniture lends an earthy stability.

A bay window overlooking the ocean floods a dining room with sunlight. Pillows add a fire element and a large circular table represents earth energy.

Layered white on walls, ceiling, and easily maintainable outdoor fabric integrate a living space as it eliminates perimeters and establishes room-to-room perspectives.

This Serengeti savanna is home to an untold number of animals, so it conjures up many of the refuge aspects of the earth element.

This shot I took of the sensuous curves of a windswept dune in the Thar Desert in Rajasthan, India, often comes to mind when I begin to design an earth space.

Gray Marble 530-4

Field Poppy 1195-7   Roasted Chestnut 15-30

Paneled walls, left, provide a solid backdrop for collections of porcelain and photography; dark taupe grass cloth, right, covers the wall behind several figurative statues.

Cordovan cowhides strewn across dark stained floors focus the furnishings; sand-colored leather upholstery modifies the overt air aspect of a loft's oversized windows.

Cornucopia 1203-7

Primal textures exemplify earth's richness. Left, bronze mirrors and an altar table above a python veneered cabinet; right, scholar's rocks, moss, carved wood, and marble.

Upholstery that mixes leather with wool, grainy wooden stools, a tailored sisal rug, and a predominantly taupe decor lend character to a generic, cube-shaped room.

Kangaroo 1078-4

In earth terms, comfort is associated with clearly delineated, enclosed spaces. Left, nineteenth-century painted panels cocoon a dining room; right, a nest-like reading nook in a Swiss chalet.

Greyhound 1008-3

Paneled walls, plenty of bookcases, and earth-toned upholstery align a Swiss chalet's interior with striking views of pine trees and mountain ranges. A roaring hearth supplies the fire element.

Sensual clay tones, inviting furniture, and a stone floor insert demarcate an intimate space in a cavernous room at the Liberty National Golf Club.

A wood panel with ellipses that resembles an abstract tree-scape divides a kitchen from a deep-seated sofa in a Westchester house, while a stone floor throughout is relational.

Chocolate Ripple 1078-7   Stone's Throw 1008-7

Grandly proportioned spaces acquire intimacy with grass cloth and upholstery in warm taupes, left, and with a nineteenth-century Chinese carpet and rich, large-scale paintings, right.

An ebony-stained floor, cowhide carpet, and textured wood furniture balance floor-to-ceiling windows and neutralize any traces of isolation that can crop up in spaces where air dominates.

A charcoal curved wall encloses a dining banquette; a dark brown floor coalesces furniture in styles from nineteenth-century Portuguese to mid-century modern.

I acknowledged the air element in a living room by floating a painting in front of a window, but then I tempered it with aged woods, patina-coated surfaces, and graphic furniture silhouettes.

I offset the extreme earthiness of a carpeted, paneled room by bringing in air, fire, and water in the guise of a spontaneous-looking arrangement of shapely white furniture.

Layering, in decor terms an earth feature, is achieved here with framed bark cloth, a mahogany cabinet, a skirted leather ottoman, and weathered Ethiopian chairs.

Three means of entry left this kitchen feeling like an undetermined through-space until I anchored the island with shapely legs, hung an oversized pendant, and installed wood cabinetry.

This consummately earthy kitchen has French doors that access a garden, a Chinese screen, wood floors bordered by Jerusalem stone, and oak cabinets.

A fiery Sputnik chandelier energizes a casually formal, tranquil setting where upholstered walls and a mix of banquettes and wingback chairs encircle a lime-rubbed oak table.

ACKNOWLEDGMENTS

Heartfelt thanks to the following people. This monograph would not have been possible without their help, support, energy, and commitment. Sophie Antonopoulos, who took my photographs and patiently gave them some cohesion. Linda O'Keeffe, who wrote such poetic words. Sam Shahid and Matthew Kraus, who created such masterful art direction. Charles Miers and Kathleen Jayes at Rizzoli, who pushed me to do this book. Jill Cohen, my literary agent, who made it all possible. The many publications that continue to support my work and where many of the images that now appear in this book were originally published: *Architectural Digest, Elle Décor, House Beautiful, Interior Design, Luxe, Milieu, New York Spaces, New York Times,* and *Veranda*, which kindly allowed me to use the image that now graces the book's cover. My wonderful clients whose ongoing trust allows me to be creative every day. My loyal staff—Maureen Martin, David Rogal, John Mistriotis, Devin Hines, Lindsey Reese, Kerry Perchaluk, Natalia Ramirez, Dorcia Kelley, Trudi Romeo, and Tom Wetjen – who are all as responsible for the projects in this book as much as I am. Special thanks to Pittsburgh Paint (PPG) for their support.

First published in the United States of America in 2016
by Rizzoli International Publications, Inc.
300 Park Avenue South
New York, NY 10010
www.rizzoliusa.com

Poetry on page 109 © Sanober Khan, reprinted with permission.

DESIGNED BY SAM SHAHID
Art Director: Matthew Kraus

All photography by Vicente Wolf

2016 2017 2018 2019 / 10 9 8 7 6 5 4 3 2 1

Distributed in the U.S. trade by Random House, New York

Printed in China

ISBN-13: 978-0-8478-4815-7

Library of Congress Catalog Control Number: 2015957136